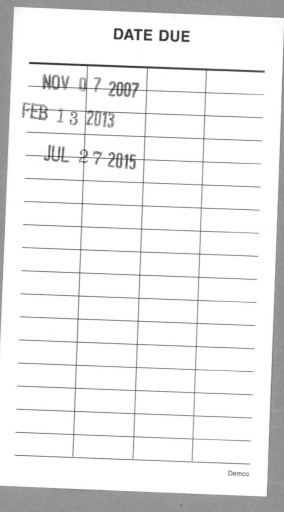

Pond

GORDON MORRISON

Houghton Mifflin Company Boston 2002

Walter Lorraine Books

To Deborah of the Sudbury
who shares the joy and wonder in nature and art

Walter Lorraine *wl* Books

Library of Congress Cataloging-in-Publication Data
Morrison, Gordon.
  Pond / by Gordon Morrison.
      p. cm.
Summary: Observes how a glacial pond and the abundance of plants and
animals that draw life from it change over the course of a year.
  ISBN 0-618-10271-X
  1. Pond animals—Juvenile literature. 2. Ponds—Juvenile literature.
[1. Pond animals. 2. Pond plants. 3. Ponds.] I. Title.
  QL146.3 .M67 2002
  577.63'6—dc21

                                                    2002003494

Printed in the United States of America
PHR 10 9 8 7 6 5 4 3 2 1

A gentle rain has fallen all night.
A stream fills with the rainfall and flows out of the woods into a pond.
Snow is melting, and ice is turning back into pond water.
Warmer days are returning to the pond. Winter is giving way to spring.

Some marsh plants:
Cattails grow to 9 feet, in
shallows and at water's edge.

Bulrushes grow to 8 feet
tall, in deeper shallows.

Sedges grow to 3½ feet
tall, on wet edges.

Marsh: an area of shallow, slow-moving
water, where mostly tall,
grasslike plants grow.

Several weeks pass, and the days are a little warmer. Today red-winged blackbirds return to the pond, a sure sign that spring is near. The male blackbirds return first. They gather in a marsh of cattail plants. In a few days the females will return. The males will put on a noisy show to attract them, calling *kon-ka-reeee, kon-ka-reeee* from old cattail stalks.

Under water near the base of the cattail plants young caddisfly insects slowly crawl. Young caddisflies build cases around themselves for safety. The cases are made from bits of leaves, twigs, or sand found in the pond. So caddisflies may be hard to see.

 Caddisfly young, or larva.

 A larva produces glue to bond a ring of material around its head.

As more rings are bonded together, they are pushed back

until its body is covered in a case.

Larvae live eleven months before leaving the water as adults. Adults mate and lay eggs, living only days or weeks.

Spring has arrived.
The buds of many trees
and shrubs are growing,
adding a touch of spring
color around the pond.
But the red maple trees
are the first to bloom.
They have already opened
their red buds and flowers.

While the days get warm,
spring nights remain cold.
A morning mist drifts across the pond.

A pair of wood ducks arrives at
the pond. The female lands on a
tree near the edge of a swamp area.
Her colorful mate watches her.
She is looking at a hole in the tree.
It will make a good place for a nest.
The wood ducks will stay and raise a family.

Some swamp trees:
Red maples grow to 80 feet
and have red-winged seeds.

Yellow birches grow to
80 feet. They have yellow
peeling bark and cones.

White cedars reach about
45 feet. They are evergreens
with small cones.

Swamp: an area of shallow, still water where mostly trees and shrubs grow.

Air, moisture, and mist:
Warm, moist air is light and rises.
Cold, drier air is heavy and falls.

Spring days warm the pond.
Spring nights cool the land.

When moist pond air rises, dry land air falls to replace it. Where the cold and warm air mix, the moisture forms a mist.

This is only one way mist forms.

A turtle pokes its head through
the pond's surface.
It is a painted turtle.
It just dug itself out of
the mud in the bottom
of the pond, where it
spent the cold
winter months.

Some pond turtles:
Painted turtle grows to 8 inches
long. It is our most common turtle.

Spotted turtle grows to 5 inches. It is
rare. Older ones have many yellow spots.

Snapping turtle can reach 3 feet long.
North America's largest turtle, unlike
most, cannot withdraw into its shell.

Turtle ancestors roamed the
earth even before the dinosaurs.

Around the same time the turtle appears,
a frog digs out from its winter place.
It is a green frog. It spent the
winter buried in a muddy bank.

Some pond frogs:
Green frog, to 4 inches long.
Its call, *t-chung,* sounds like an old banjo.
The male's eardrum, or tympanum, is
larger than its eye and has a yellow spot.

Bullfrog grow to 8 inches.
It is the largest North American frog.
Its call is a deep *jug-o-rum, jug-o-rum.*

Leopard frog, to 4 inches long. An individual frog
may change its color from tan, when in a dry
habitat, to green when in a wet one.

Frog life cycle:
Tadpoles hatch from eggs that are
only $1/16$ inch in size.
Tadpoles breathe through gills.

They eat ooze, the layer on the
pond bottom made up of the remains
of minute plants and animals.

Reaching 3 inches in a year, they grow
hind legs, then front legs. Their eyes
move to the top of their head, and their
nostrils and lungs develop for
air breathing. Their tail shrinks.

Three more years pass before
the frogs are adults.

During the past three or four weeks, female red-winged blackbirds have been very busy. They have built nests and laid eggs. The males guard the nest area while the females sit on their eggs. Then three days ago the baby birds hatched.

Young blackbirds eat a lot and grow fast. In about a week they will be able to fly. While they grow they must be very careful not to fall from the nest. There are many dangers, like the large water snake prowling nearby.

Northern water snakes can grow to 3 feet or more. They are excellent swimmers. Their color varies, but older snakes are dark.

They eat frogs, insects, birds, eggs, young turtles, and fish.

As many as 30 live young are born at once. Water snakes group together to hibernate through winter.

As the days continue to get warmer, yellow pond lilies bloom.
Their oval leaves, called lily pads, float on the surface.
Snails crawl, upside down, across the bottom of the lily pads.
The snails are eating tiny animals called moss animals.
The moss animals are eating very tiny plants
called green algae. The algae cover the bottom
of the lily pads in a slimy coat.

Whirligig beetles whirl in circles around
the lily pads. Whirligigs have four eyes.
They see above and below the water
at the same time. They carry air
bubbles under water to breathe.

Mussels live on the bottom of the
pond. They take food called
plankton from the pond water.
Plankton looks like dust
drifting through the water.
Sometimes mussels move, *very slowly,*
and leave tracks in the mud.

Freshwater snail: a small animal with a
shell about 1 inch long, into which it
withdraws for safety. Snails are food
for fish, ducks, muskrats, and turtles.

Moss animals: very small animals
that may form colonies, which look
like moss. Their tentacles draw in
algae and plankton.

Green algae: simple green plants.
There are many forms, from
this microscopic form to
the 2-foot-tall sea lettuce.

Some pond insects:
Whirligig beetle, to ½ inch.
It can dive or fly to escape
or to catch other insects.

Water strider, body to ½ inch.
Its shadow may be easier to see
than the insect walking on water.

Two look-alikes:
Water boatman, ¾ inch.
Swims upright in a jerking motion,
rowing with four hind legs.
Backswimmer, ½ inch. Swims
on its back in a steadier motion,
rowing with two hind legs.

Freshwater mussels grow to 4 inches.
To move, mussels reach out with their
foot, then pull their body forward.
Count the darker ridges on the
shell to find how old a mussel is.

Plankton: tiny and microscopic
plants and animals that drift within
the water. They are food for snails,
fish, insects, and others.

It's been six weeks since the wood ducks came to the pond. About four weeks ago the female laid her eggs. Yesterday twelve downy chicks hatched. Today their mother calls for them to leave the nest. Using sharp claws on their toes, they climb to the nest opening. They leap from the tree and tumble into the water. Unhurt, the ducklings swim away with their mother. She will take good care of her ducklings.

By late spring the flowers of the
red maple trees have fallen.
Their red fruits have grown
and their leaves are spreading.
Nearby, shrubs of sweet
pepperbush spread their
leaves, while shrubs of
blueberries open their
flowers and their leaves.
In the pond new
cattail leaves grow
out of the water.

Days pass and plants continue to grow. Young dragonflies, called nymphs, crawl up cattail leaves and into shrubs. Grasping the plants, they break free from their outer skin, then unfold and spread their new wings. Finally they are adult dragonflies. And, in a flash, they are flying and hunting along the pond's edge.

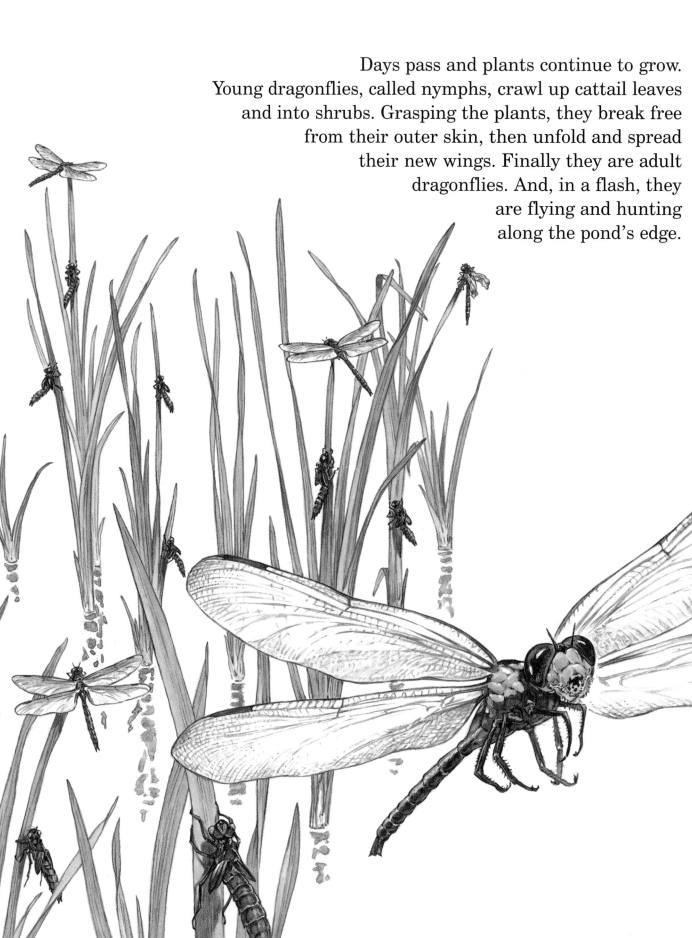

SPLASH!
A bird dives into the pond. It's a belted kingfisher. It has caught a fish and is now flying out of the water.
The kingfisher flies to a dead tree, eats the fish, then watches for more fish to catch.
Belted kingfishers are excellent fishermen.

Dragonfly nymph, to 1 inch. Lives under water and grabs prey with its huge hinged jaws.

Dragonfly, up to 4 inches long. It has a heavy body and holds its wings out from its sides. The damselfly, a smaller relative, holds its wings parallel to its slender body.

During the days of the dinosaurs, giant dragonfly ancestors flew on wings 2 feet across.

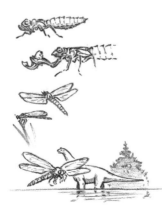

Belted kingfisher, 14 inches long. Males have only one blue "belt."

Watching fish, the kingfisher hovers, then dives, plunging headfirst into the pond.

Its nest is a burrow, usually 3–6 feet deep, dug into a sloped bank.

In early summer, painted turtles and green frogs lay their eggs. Turtles lay up to twelve eggs in a hole they dig in the woods. By late summer young turtles hatch. Newly hatched turtles look just like adults, only much smaller. Somehow they know which way to crawl to get to the pond.

How the pond may have formed: 12,000 years ago the earth was in a cold period. A glacier, a half mile thick, covered this area. As it grew it pushed and carried rocks, sand, soil, and other debris with it, carving and shaping the land into ridges and hollows.

When the earth warmed, the glacier started to melt. The water melting from the ice washed down the ridges and hollows, carrying debris with it. Some debris washed into a pile at the end of a large hollow, forming a wall.

After the glacier melted, the wall acted as a dam. It held some of the water in the hollow. As time passed, plants grew around the water's edge and up the slopes of the ridges.

Over thousands of years, many changes took place. Many kinds of plants and animals came and went. Slowly the ridges became woodland hills, and different habitats formed around the water's edge. And the hollow became the pond it is today.

Green frogs lay thousands of eggs on the pond's surface. In about four days tiny tadpoles hatch and swim away. Tadpoles look more like fish than frogs. Many frog eggs may be eaten before they hatch.

How the pond gets its water today: Clouds carry moisture from other places and drop rain and snow into the pond.

Runoff, water from rain or melting snow, flows off the land into the pond.

Groundwater, water that sinks into the soil, moves to the pond underground.

Some groundwater sinks deep and may become part of an underground stream.

A spring may gush from the stream into the pond's bottom.

An upland stream carries its water and runoff into the pond.

How the pond loses water: Wind, cold, and heat take moisture from the pond. Hot summer days take the most pond water. Moisture rising from the pond forms clouds, and it is carried away.

Water soaks into the soil under the pond and may be carried away in underground streams.

Water flows out from a downland stream.

Plants in and around the pond draw water, and animals drink from it to survive.

Pond or lake?
A pond is usually small in size, with shallow, warm water.
Sunlight reaches to the pond bottom, and plants grow from shore to shore.

A lake may be large or small in surface area, with deep, cold water.
Sunlight does not reach to the lake bottom, so plants are on the shore only; none are on the bottom.

By midsummer the days are hot, and the pond water is getting warm. Cattail plants have grown to more than six feet tall. Animals visit the pond. Deer eat the water plants, and raccoons hunt for fish, mussels, frogs, and turtles.

Tree swallows fly over and around the pond. They catch insects in the air
and drink from the pond's surface. The young wood ducks are growing,
and the father duck has molted, shedding his colorful feathers.
New, plain feathers grow in their place.
The blueberry fruits are ripe. And sweet pepperbush
flowers fill the air with their spicy scent.

Suddenly an owl swoops down on the wood ducks.
The ducks scatter, swimming as fast as they can
to the protection of nearby plants.
It is a barred owl. It swoops down again and again.
Many weeks ago the owl caught several young ducklings.
But now the young ducks are eight weeks old, full grown
and ready to fly. They are just too hard to catch.
Finally the barred owl gives up and flies back into the swamp.

Barred owl, 21 inches tall. It gets its name from the barred feather pattern that sweeps across its upper breast.

This owl nests in a tree hollow in a swamp or thick woods. It raises two to four young, and may hunt in the daytime. It eats mostly mice, but also frogs, insects, birds, snakes, and young ducks and muskrats.

Its call sounds like *Who cooks for you? Who cooks for you-a-a-all?*

The summer days are hot and the pond's water is warm.
The shallow water is now warm enough for pumpkinseed sunfish to lay their eggs.
The male makes the nest by moving pebbles and sticks away with his mouth.
He then shapes a depression by fanning the area with his fins. After the
female sunfish lays her eggs, the male guards them. Sunfish will
swim across the nest and fan it with their fins. This brings fresh
water to the eggs and keeps underwater debris out of the nest.

Aquatic, or water, plants live in the pond.
Pickerel weed and arrowhead grow out of the water.
The white water lilies' round lily pads float on the surface.
Underwater plants of coontail and waterweed
make good hiding places for growing tadpoles
and young sunfish after they hatch.

Some pond fish:
Pumpkinseed sunfish, to 8 inches.
The male makes a nest when
the water temperature
reaches 68 degrees.

Largemouth bass, to 18 inches.
This relative of the sunfish
is found among plants.

Chain pickerel, to 24 inches.
It lives in shallows and swamps.

Minnows, to 2½ inches.
These are not baby fish,
though their small size may make
them appear to be babies. They
swim in schools in shallow waters.

During the summer months the red-winged blackbirds have raised
a second family, and the young wood ducks have become good fliers.
The blackbirds are full grown now. They gather together to eat
insects and seeds, while the wood ducks grow stronger by flying circles
around the pond. They are all getting ready to leave the pond. Summer is ending.

A muskrat swims across the pond. It leaves a straight slice through the water's
surface. Only the dark tip of its head can be seen above the water.

Muskrat: one of the largest and most aquatic rodents. About 24 inches long, including a 10-inch flattened, rudderlike tail.

Muskrats eat mostly plants, including all parts of cattails, but they also eat frogs, turtles, snails, mussels, fish, and insects.

Lodge: the muskrats' home is made from leaves and stalks of cattails and other marsh plants. (Beaver lodges are made from tree branches and limbs.) They raise two to three families a year, with six to seven young in each litter.

Fall has arrived. Plants are changing color.
The plants around the pond change color first.
Red maple leaves turn blazing red.
Blueberry leaves turn yellow and red, then crimson.
Sweet pepperbush leaves turn yellow and ochre.

Fall days may be cold, but a few dragonflies still hunt.
A few turtles still lie in the sun, white water lilies still bloom.
And whirligig beetles turn slow circles on the pond's surface.

The noisy chatter and chirping of the blackbirds is heard around the pond.
It is time for them to fly south for the winter. At first only a few birds fly
into the sky. Then others join them, flying out of the
cattail marsh and up from the shrubs and trees.
They form a flock and fly away.
In a few minutes they are gone
and the pond is quiet.

A muskrat adds cattail leaves and stalks to
its lodge, making it stronger and thicker.
It is preparing for winter.
Muskrats live in the pond all year.
The lodge is their home.
It protects them from danger
and cold winter weather.

Another month passes. The days are colder.
The wood ducks have flown south
to a warmer place.
Frogs and turtles have dug into
the mud. The muskrats store
cattail roots in their lodge.
The pond begins to freeze.

Water and ice:
Water, like all things, is made
of tiny parts called molecules.

The molecules of all things
expand (move apart) when
heated, and contract (move
together) when cooled.

But at 39 degrees, water
molecules begin to expand
again, and at 32 degrees
they stop moving and
bond (freeze) together,
leaving empty spaces. The
spaces make the solid (ice)
lighter than the liquid (water)
around it, so the ice floats.

It's now winter, and the pond is frozen. The ice grows a little thicker every day. A small flock of birds moves through the shrubs. Black-capped chickadees, tufted titmice, and a downy woodpecker are foraging, looking for food. They will find lots of seeds and fruits around the pond.

Winter below the ice:
Plants wilt, but most seeds and roots survive.
Fish and some insects are active, but move
more slowly. Mussels and snails are sometimes
active. A turtle may dig out of the mud. Muskrats
may gulp air from trapped bubbles if they leave the lodge.

Ice helps insulate the pond from freezing to the bottom.

The winter wind blows snow into patterns and drifts across the ice. Dry cattail plants rustle in the wind. All seems still. But tracks in the snow show that animals still visit.

In about a month the gentle rains will come.
The ice will melt into the pond. The blackbirds will return.
And the pond, once again, will fill with activity and life.